Belsay Hall, Castle and Gardens

Roger White

Introduction

The Belsay that visitors see today comprises three distinct but related elements: a medieval castle that was enlarged in the early 17th century, a Greek Revival mansion that superseded it as a family residence at the beginning of the 19th century and an outstanding garden linking the two buildings, much of which was created out of the quarries that supplied the stone for the new house.

Belsay is the creation of the Middleton family, over more than seven centuries. The Middletons were first recorded as owning Belsay in 1270 and although they moved out of the hall in 1962, the estate that surrounds the historic nucleus of hall, castle and garden remains in their possession. The great fortified tower that still dominates the castle was built both as a statement of family pride and as a response to the conflict and unrest in this border region between England and Scotland. It was then extended into a rambling country house after the union of the two kingdoms under King James I in 1603 brought relative peace. The Middletons lived in the castle until the completion in 1817 of the new mansion, which was designed by the then owner Sir Charles Monck (1779–1867).

Belsay Hall was inspired by what Sir Charles had seen on his extended honeymoon in Greece and is a building of austere perfection. Under the terms of the guardianship agreement by which it passed to the care of the government in 1980, the hall is displayed without furnishings, revealing to visitors the fine craftsmanship that went into its construction.

Contrasting with the strict geometry of the hall, and linking it with the castle, Sir Charles Monck's quarry garden is a remarkable example of the Picturesque style with a microclimate that makes it possible to grow tender plants beyond their normal northern limit.

Above: Sir Charles Monck (1779–1867), who designed Belsay Hall and Gardens, as a young man

Facing page: Belsay Castle
Previous page: The great arch in the quarry garden

Tour of the Hall

Belsay Hall was a modern villa with a comfortable library, drawing room and dining room built to overlook a romantic prospect to the south. But its owner, Sir Charles Monck, was obsessed by ancient Greece and owned every book published on Greek architecture. So the details inside and out were derived from the Classical buildings which he had seen on his honeymoon in Athens. Work began on the house in 1807 and finished in 1817.

FOLLOWING THE TOUR

The tour of the hall starts in the stable block and follows a suggested route through all parts of the building open to the public. Tours of the gardens and castle follow on pages 20 and 28. Small numbered plans in the margins highlight key points on the tour of the hall.

STABLE BLOCK

The stables are a large U-shaped block, built, like the hall, from a handsome sandstone quarried on the estate. They were designed by Sir Charles Monck between 1807 and 1817 and his drawings indicate the uses of the various rooms. As well as stalls for the horses, there was a saddle room, coach house, dry and wet laundries, hay chamber, malt chamber and brewery (though the last was in fact never used as such). The stable block now contains the state coach of the High Sheriff of Northumberland, which was built in the 1850s by Atkinson & Philipson of Newcastle and is on loan from Northumberland County Council. Made to take the High Sheriff to meet the Assize Judges during Assizes Week, it was last used in 1906. Its presence at Belsay is particularly appropriate, since between 1423 and 1884 no fewer than eight members of the Middleton family held this ancient office.

The stable block was sited here partly to shield the house from cold north-easterly winds. The main front faces south and forms a fine composition with the hall. It too is in an austere Greek Revival style, with a broad pediment to the end of each wing and an octagonal clock-tower rising above the centre, the design of which was inspired by the Tower of the Winds in Athens.

During the Second World War the hall was requisitioned for military use and the stables were used by the Army as billets for the soldiers. They slept on straw palliasses, with boots for pillows and literally head to toe, as there were so many of them. The officers were billeted in the hall. The area that is now the car park was used as the drill square, where the soldiers paraded each morning. Cooking was done outside as there was no proper cookhouse and soldiers washed and shaved using water from the taps and rough sinks in the yard.

SITE OF THE CHAPEL

Between the stables and the hall the grassy mound planted with trees is the site of a chapel that was taken down at some time in the early 19th century. It was probably the Presbyterian chapel built by the nonconformist Middletons in the 17th century and was abandoned after Sir Charles conformed to the Church of England in the early 19th century.

Left: A 19th-century photograph of the Tower of the Winds (150–100 BC) in Athens, the inspiration for the clock-tower of Belsay's stable block
Below: The south front of the stable block

Facing page: Detail of the brass balustrade and columns of the Pillar Hall gallery

5

BELSAY HALL'S SETTING

Until the building of the new hall, the park and gardens at Belsay naturally focused on the castle. All this changed in the early 19th century when Sir Charles Monck cleared away the village that lay to the south-west of the castle and rebuilt it much further east, out of sight of the hall, on the main road from Newcastle to Jedburgh. The entrance front on the east side of the hall looks over a ha-ha, or concealed ditch, to parkland with groups of trees, apparently set at random but in fact carefully placed by Sir Charles so that the house was largely screened from the view of visitors approaching along the main drive (now lost).

He intended to 'improve' the view eastwards by extending the small Belsay Lough into a much larger lake but after protests from villagers that it would be dangerously close to them, he made a new lake to the south instead. The boathouse that was to have stood on the banks of the enlarged Belsay Lough can still be seen today from the drive to the north of the hall, stranded in a field.

On the south side of the mansion Sir Charles created two descending formal terraces supported on a massive arcaded wall, the upper one with close-mown grass and the lower one with geometric flower beds. On the far side of the new lake to the south, the steep, rocky hillside was planted with a mixture of then newly introduced exotic conifers, Scots pines and native hardwoods.

Top: Sir Arthur Middleton's children in about 1890
Above: Mary Middleton, Sir Arthur's daughter-in-law, with two of her children, on the lake in about 1916
Left: View of Belsay Hall from the south-east, in Country Life, 1940

Facing page: The entrance front at night, in Country Life, 1940

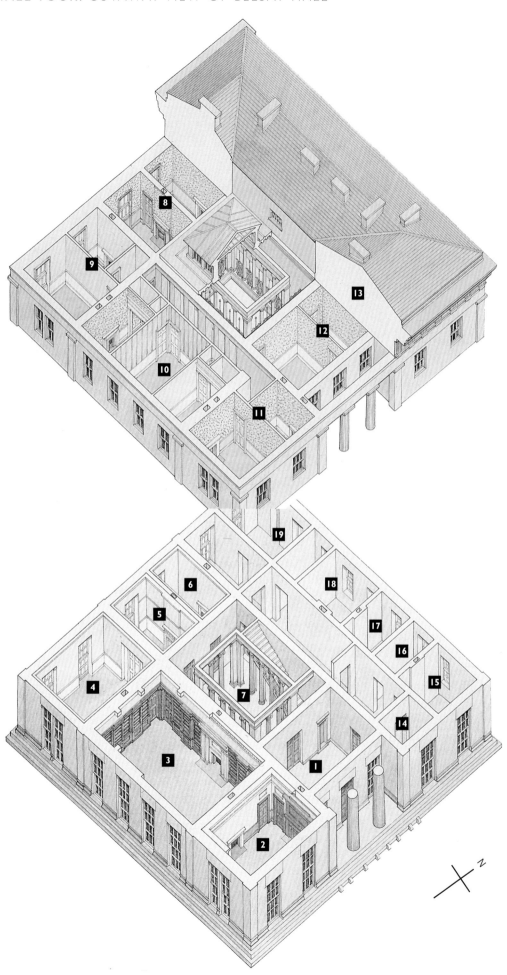

THE HALL

1 Entrance hall

2 Study

3 Library

4 Dining room

5 Anteroom

6 Housekeeper's room

7 Pillar Hall

8 West bedrooms

9 Nurseries

10 South bedrooms

11 East bedrooms

12 East bedrooms

13 North rooms
(not open to the public)

14 Telephone room

15 Estate office

16 Water closet

17 Butler's pantry

18 Servants' hall

19 Kitchen

EXTERIOR AND ENTRANCE FRONT

The severe exterior of Belsay Hall resembles a stone box. The four facades of the house, though identical in size and shape, are all different in detail and, in a clockwise direction from the entrance front on the east to the service front on the north, become progressively less elaborate. The house, constructed of a beautiful honey-coloured sandstone flecked with tiny pieces of iron ore, is exactly 100ft square (30m square), and, like a Greek temple, it sits on a crepidoma, or stepped plinth (the steps are each 1ft, or 0.3m, high). Everything – the dimensions, the proportions, the masonry detail – was worked out by Sir Charles with mathematical precision: the proportional ratios were calculated to three decimal places.

The house appears to consist of just two storeys, but in fact there are also a concealed basement and attic, the latter contained within the shallow-pitched roof and lit from a light-well invisible from the exterior. The functional north front of the service area, which would not have been seen by visitors arriving along the main drive, is completely plain and has three storeys as well as a basement.

All the facades are subdivided into three sections by giant pilasters, complemented by the massive Doric entablature, the crowning cornice of which projects 3ft (1m). The ground- and first-floor windows are set into the walls without any mouldings, emphasising the minimalist quality of this style.

At the centre of the east front, unmistakably announcing the entrance to the house, there is a portico *in antis*, that is, set into the building rather than projecting, as was more usual on a country house. The two 20ft (6m) high columns were copied from an ancient temple in Athens known as the Theseion (449–444 BC), which seems to have been Sir Charles's favourite Greek building. Each column at Belsay is constructed from blocks of stone assembled without mortar, with joints so fine that it is said that a pen-knife cannot be inserted between them. The fluting was carved after the columns had been constructed. Within the portico the high, sheer stone walls appear rather intimidating.

Left: Belsay Hall from the east: the entrance front is dominated by the portico, its two columns copied from the Theseion (449–444 BC) in Athens

▌ ENTRANCE HALL

The austerity and precision of the exterior is carried through to the entrance hall, which has unplastered stone walls and a coffered ceiling, made of plaster but imitating stone. These create the impression that the visitor has indeed entered an ancient temple. Three plain door frames are incised into the stonework. Straight ahead are double doors leading into the central Pillar Hall, flanked by fireplaces designed to look like temple doors.

The door to the right gives access to the service side of the house, as well as to Sir Charles Monck's study and the estate office and telephone room of his grandson and successor, Sir Arthur Middleton (1838–1933). The tour proceeds to the left, into the three reception rooms on the south side of the building.

▌ STUDY

This room was originally the dining room, as is indicated by the large sideboard to the left as you come through the door. In 1909 it became the study of Sir Arthur Middleton. Like all the reception rooms it is spacious and filled with light from the large windows. The detail is sparing but scholarly and, of course, without any furniture, the interiors seem stark. The rooms are known to have been almost entirely furnished with restrained late-Georgian pieces made for the house when it was built, mainly by the estate carpenter William White of Stamfordham. Some slightly more elaborate items were probably bought from the well-known firm Gillows of Lancaster; even so, the overall effect would always have been quite reticent. During the Second World War, when the hall was requisitioned, the Army used this room as an office.

▌ LIBRARY

Occupying the centre of the south front and not fitted up until 1828, this is the most impressive of the reception rooms, and the one apparently most often used by the family. As such it is a good example of the 'social' library that superseded the more 'scholarly' library in late 18th-century country houses, although there is no doubt that Sir Charles Monck stocked the shelves with serious volumes – among them, every book then published on the architecture of Greece.

Top: Drawings for the frieze in the library, probably by Sir Charles Monck
Centre: The sideboard in the study, formerly the dining room
Below: Elinor Middleton (1876–1942), Sir Arthur Middleton's daughter, in the library, 1911

The design of the oak bookcases lining the walls was based, on a reduced scale, on the measurements that Sir Charles had made of the Erechtheion (421–405 BC), a temple on the Acropolis in Athens. The design continues into the handsome chimneypiece of yellow scagliola (imitation marble) and white marble; this and the alabaster vases that formerly sat on top of the bookcases were supplied by Michali & Co of Leghorn (Livorno) in Italy. Around the room, below the very simple beamed ceiling, is a typical Greek Revival frieze composed of a band of anthemion, or stylised honeysuckle, above one of 'Greek key' pattern. When furnished with Regency chairs, sofas and tables in mahogany or rosewood, with the shelves filled with books and the floor covered by Turkey carpets, it must have been an extremely pleasant room. Many former staff recall dances here in the early 20th century. The family took afternoon tea here at 4.30pm every day and coffee was also served here after lunch. In the period between the wars, the Middleton children played card games here in the evening and used the room as base when playing hide-and-seek.

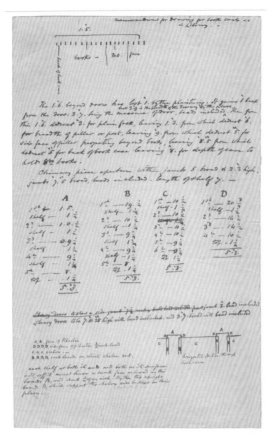

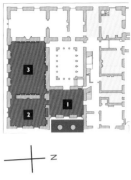

Left: Sir Charles Monck's measurements of the Erechtheion (421–405 BC) in Athens, used as the basis for the design of the library bookcases
Below: The library as shown in Country Life, 1940

Serving the hall

Although the hours were long and the work hard, former staff remember happy times in service at Belsay, sunbathing on the roof above the Pillar Hall and enjoying outings at Christmas

Country houses such as Belsay required an army of staff to maintain them and to cater for the needs of the family. The position and roles of each member of the domestic staff were clearly defined in a strict hierarchy, from the butler and housekeeper at the top to the scullery maid at the bottom. In 1930 the indoor staff at Belsay included no fewer than 12 maids and manservants, including a chauffeur, butler, footman, housekeeper, housemaids, kitchen-maids, a lady's-maid and a sewing-maid. With the exception of nannies and nurserymaids, who would have slept in the nursery with the small children, those who 'lived in' were – in Sir Charles Monck's time – accommodated on the second floor. In the 1880s, when Sir Arthur Middleton altered the layout of the rooms, a mezzanine floor was inserted between the ground and first floors in the service wing – this is clearly visible from the corridor near the top of the cellar steps. Kitchen-maids and parlour-maids then slept in the rooms on this floor, while housemaids remained on the second floor. Although the hours were long and the work hard, former staff remember happy times in service at Belsay: watching unnoticed as guests arrived for balls and parties, enjoying the annual outing at Christmas and sunbathing on the roof above the Pillar Hall in summer in their precious free time.

Dinah (far left) and Jane Warwick, daughter and mother, who worked as laundrymaids at Belsay after the First World War

4 DINING ROOM

This room was originally intended as the drawing room and an early plan shows it opening into the smaller room to the north (now the anteroom) via a screen of columns. As the family often used the library as a drawing room, this room served instead as a garden room. It seems not to have been properly fitted out until 1912, as part of a large programme of redecoration carried out by Sir Arthur Middleton. It was then turned into the main dining room, linked by mahogany double doors to the adjoining anteroom. It is probable that Sir Arthur changed the function of this room because of his obsession with hot food. Former staff recalled how he would test the temperature of his meals with a thermometer to ensure that they were hot enough. As this room was in the south-west corner of the hall, it was closer to the service areas, and so food did not have to be carried far from the kitchen.

The work on the hall in 1912, by Robson & Sons of Newcastle to designs by W H Knowles, entailed the removal of the old windows, the installation of new floorboards, chimneypiece and panelled ceiling and the plastering of the bare stone walls. Sir Arthur, who had studied his grandfather's plans closely, provided the details of the frieze and mouldings. The chimneypiece is made of white marble and has Doric columns. The picture rails (a wooden one at low level and a brass one higher up) may have been closely hung with paintings. These were sold at auction in 1962.

5 ANTEROOM AND
6 HOUSEKEEPER'S ROOM

Sir Charles Monck intended the anteroom to be part of a large drawing room, entered directly from the central Pillar Hall. It became a separate room only in 1912. The room next to the anteroom was originally intended as a smoking room but in about 1887–8 it became the housekeeper's room. A screen was inserted to create a passage that gave access between the dining room in the south-west corner of the hall and the service wing that runs along the north side of the house. In its present condition the room reflects the changes through which it has passed, with decorative plasterwork remaining from the different phases of its use.

*Sir Arthur Middleton
(1838–1933) who inherited
the house from his
grandfather in 1867 and
changed the function of one
of the main rooms due to his
obsession with hot food*

13

7 PILLAR HALL

Occupying the centre of the house, this splendid two-storey hall is the architectural climax of Belsay. It is meant to evoke the open-roofed atrium, or central courtyard, of a classical villa – a Roman architectural precedent rather than a Greek one. The Northumberland climate meant that it had to be roofed, with natural lighting provided by roof lights and a clerestory, or upper level of windows. The Pillar Hall functioned both as a reception room and as a circulation space, giving access to the different parts of the house. On the ground floor are closely spaced Ionic columns, with Doric columns on the floor above – a reversal of the usual arrangement in classical buildings. Sir William Gell – another architecturally inclined gentleman whom Sir Charles Monck met in Athens – made an alternative design proposing that instead of columns the upper floor should have caryatids, or carved female figures, such as occur on the porch of the Erechtheion on the Acropolis. But it is said that Sir Charles felt that they would look too clumsy if carved from local sandstone by local masons. Everything is nevertheless executed in stone: floor, walls, columns and even the ceilings of the colonnade and stairs. All the detail derives from authentic Greek precedent. The elegant Ionic capitals proved too tricky for Sir Charles to draw and for this he may have employed the young John Dobson, who was to become the outstanding local architect working in the neoclassical style. A staircase behind the north colonnade leads up to the first floor; the usual solution in country houses was to place the staircase within the central well. Both the staircase and the gallery have brass balustrades designed by Sir Charles's sister Isabella, after she had seen the new staircase at Northumberland House in London, built in 1822. It seems the balustrades were not made until 1830, when Messrs William Collins, of 227 Strand, London, were paid £805 for the work. Artificial lighting at the upper level was provided by brass lamp-stands, which screwed into the top of the balustrade between each Doric column. At ground level plaster casts of statues by John Flaxman (the leading neoclassical sculptor of his day), of Greek women holding lamps, were placed between the Ionic columns.

Left: Detail of the brass balustrade in the Pillar Hall's gallery, designed by Sir Charles Monck's sister, Isabella

Facing page: The Pillar Hall – its austerity softened a little by statues, a large rug and vases on plinths, at the time it was photographed for Country Life, 1940

8 WEST BEDROOMS AND 9 NURSERIES

The visitor now ascends the stairs to the first floor. Here, the family bedrooms run around three sides of the gallery. The rooms nearest the head of the stairs look west, out to the rear lawn and to the trees sheltering the magnolia terrace. The two interconnecting rooms retain their original fireplace grates (all the other bedrooms have replacement grates dating to about 1909). The blue-flowered paper is of a type produced in the 1880s, probably by Morris & Co. When Sir Arthur's daughter-in-law Mary Middleton came to live at Belsay with her four children after the death of her husband, Hugh, in the First World War, she occupied the room close to the nursery suite in the south-west corner.

Belsay was home to several generations of children, all of whom used the day and night nurseries. The function of these rooms is instantly identified by the bars across the lower section of the windows to prevent accidents. Nannies and nurserymaids would have slept in the nurseries while the children were small and later on, on the second floor with the other staff. Noreen Lamb, the daughter of the estate cartman, who played with the Middleton children in the nursery as a child, recalled the room being full of toys. A family friend of the Middletons, Priscilla Napier, née Hayter remembered how 'the wide gallery that ran round the pillared hall ... provided an excellent track for small bicycles and tricycles.'

10 SOUTH AND 11 12 EAST BEDROOMS

The principal bedroom is in the centre of the rooms on the south side, overlooking the terraces and with views across to the rhododendron garden. As well as its commanding position, it is distinguished by a more elaborate plaster frieze and a grey marble fireplace. The wallpaper with classical ornament was probably introduced in 1909 when other changes were made in the house. The two interconnecting rooms flanking the central bedroom both have alcoves to contain a single bed or the head of a double bed. In these rooms the alcove is integrated into the lobby between the principal bedroom and the corridor. The joinery is given some distinction by the simple pilasters. Bed alcoves have a practical function in keeping cross-draughts off the sleeper's head, but they also relate to royal and aristocratic bedchambers of the 17th and 18th

Above: Stephen Middleton (1909–94) as a baby, later ninth baronet
Right: Detail of the blue-flowered bedroom wallpaper, dating from the 1880s
Below: The bed alcove in a bedroom on the south side of the hall

Facing page:
The fireplace in one of the bedrooms on the west side of the house

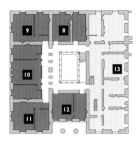

centuries. The alcoves at Belsay are in comparatively small rooms but give the bed architectural status at one end of the narrow room while freeing up the floor space for use as a private sitting room. Sir Stephen Middleton (1909–94), who inherited the title from his grandfather Sir Arthur, occupied the easterly room as an adult.

The suite in the south-east corner has the same layout as the nursery suite in the south-west. Sir Arthur occupied the larger room, which offered fine views south and east across the entrance lawns to the parkland. Elinor (1876–1942), his unmarried daughter, lived at the hall all her life and slept in the adjacent room which had once been the dressing room. The last rooms in this sequence are tucked away inside the portico and so are in the shade. When Stephen came with his mother and siblings to live here, he chose the larger bedroom.

13 NORTH ROOMS (*not open to the public*)
Doors on the east and west sides of the gallery lead through to guest rooms and a series of service stairs. Visitors to Belsay will notice that there are no bathrooms on display. Although early technology for piping water to baths and water closets was increasingly available from the 1840s, Sir Charles Monck did not incorporate either facility into the house. Later generations may have felt that alterations for bathrooms requiring visible external pipes would disrupt the aesthetics of the exterior. In any event, only the rooms on the north side, where any necessary pipework would not ruin the beauty or symmetry of the building, gained bathrooms and lavatories between 1880 and 1914. The family would have washed with jugs of water in basins or in free-standing baths, laboriously carried to and from the bedrooms by parlour-maids. Flushing lavatories were plumbed in about the time of the 1909 alterations, although the unenviable task for the housemaids of emptying bedroom chamberpots continued well into the 20th century.

The north side of the house is the only one on which the windows of the second-floor rooms are visible. The second floor (not open to the public) runs around the top of the house and is lit by windows looking into the central well above the roof of the stairs. As in many other country houses, accommodation for the servants was screened from the family rooms.

SERVICE AREA: ⑭ TELEPHONE ROOM AND ⑮ ESTATE OFFICE/STUDY

The service rooms run along the north side of the building. On the ground floor they include the telephone room, estate office/study, water closet, butler's pantry, servants' hall and kitchen. The estate office was originally Sir Charles's study or business room. Leading off the estate office/study, via an iron door, is a walk-in safe. At one point wages were handed out to staff through the window on the north side, now blocked. The telephone room next door has been known as such since the Army occupied the hall in the Second World War.

Stairs from the service corridor running west to east lead down to the cellars – four for beer, two for wine – that are cut directly into the bedrock. The servants' bells were situated halfway along the service passage, outside the butler's pantry, to alert staff when their services were required by a member of the family or a more senior member of the household staff.

Rows of coal scuttles were also lined up by parlour-maids near the butler's pantry, to ensure that fires in the rooms could be tended by the footmen. A further passage running at right angles to the main service corridor leads to the original kitchen, larder and ornamental dairy. The housekeeper's sitting room was converted in 1888 to create a more modern kitchen. Other service buildings included the gardener's room and the lamp room.

Left: John Warwick, a gardener at Belsay, photographed in about 1910
Below: Robert Best, head groom and chauffeur to the Middletons for 60 years, in the 1930s
Below left: Mr Appleby, chauffeur to the Middletons in about 1914, at the wheel of the family's Fiat car

Facing page: The staircases in the servants' quarters, in 1973

THE GARDENS

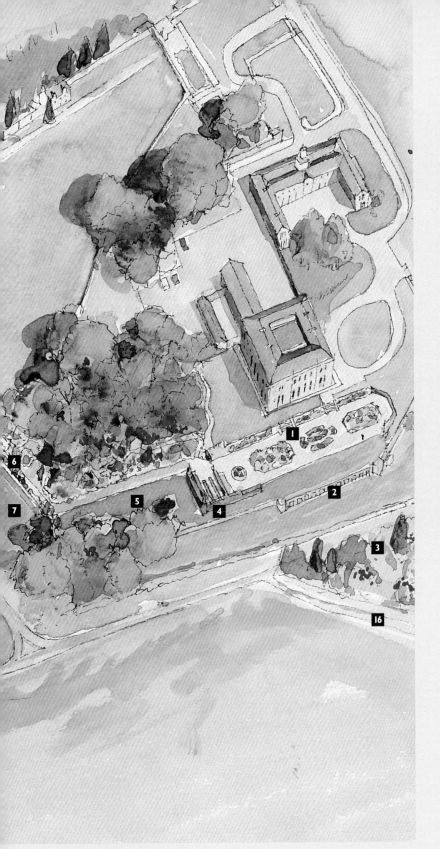

Tour of the Gardens

The layout of the Belsay gardens has remained largely unchanged since they were set out by Sir Charles Monck at the beginning of the 19th century. Monck's grandson Sir Arthur Middleton created the winter garden and yew garden but otherwise confined himself to embellishing the original design with a wider range of exotic plants and adding an extra section to the quarry. Between them the two men held the estate for an astonishing period of some 138 years, from 1795 to 1933, and since both kept meticulous records of their gardening activities, the planting history of Belsay is exceptionally well documented.

CRAG WOOD WALK

A footpath, open by kind permission of the Belsay Estate Trust, leads past the lake and around to Crag Wood. Start from **16** on the plan, then pass through a gate, keeping the lake on your right. Cross the bridge and follow the path up the stone steps, and then turn either left or right on to the circular path around the wood. Ask for details of the walk at the site shop.

ACCESS INFORMATION

There are steps leading down to the terraces. For an alternative path through the gardens, follow the signposted wheelchair route. This can be reached through the gate leading to the terraces. Please ask Belsay site staff for any further assistance.

Above: View of the quarry garden, in autumn

BELSAY'S PLANTSMEN

Both Sir Charles and Sir Arthur were keen gardeners and plantsmen. Sir Charles managed to obtain some of the earliest Douglas fir and monkey-puzzle seedlings (introduced into Britain in 1827 and 1844 respectively) and developed a revolutionary method of transplanting forest trees which he communicated to the Royal Horticultural Society. Sir Arthur was one of the first to adopt the major innovations in planting style, such as borders influenced by cottage gardens and the naturalising of daffodils in grass, that William Robinson (1838–1935) had introduced at Gravetye Manor in Sussex.

The most memorable feature, the quarry garden, was conceived by Sir Charles as a rugged and romantic contrast to the formal terraces around the hall and as a link to the abandoned medieval castle. The cutting of stone for the hall began in 1806 and it seems that Monck always intended that the resulting quarry would be developed into a garden. On a second Mediterranean tour in the 1830s he visited the ancient quarries at Siracusa in Sicily. This inspired him to develop the Belsay quarries further by constructing a towering stone arch and planting yews along the top of the quarry face so as to increase the apparent height of the sheer sides.

The underlying stone is sandstone, with the soils varying from a very sandy neutral loam overlying land-fill quarry waste on the terraces, to barely an inch or two of soil covering the levelled waste on the quarry floor. The garden receives only about 71cm (28in.) of rain each year. All plants are labelled in Latin, with a common name, if one exists, in English.

From the 1980s a massive backlog of maintenance has been tackled and the formal gardens have been restored to their appearance in the 1920s and 1930s (together with the hall and castle, they were recorded in *Country Life* in 1940). In the quarries and informal parts the plantings made by Sir Arthur at the turn of the 20th century are now fully mature. The aim here has been to maintain that effect through the use of exotic plants, while Sir Arthur's west quarry, which had reverted to scrub, will continue to house purely native plants in order to show the style of the quarry garden before the exotic introductions.

Plant Collections

The late spring-flowering pocket-handkerchief tree and the snowbell are just two of the more unusual trees in the quarry garden. Iris in the *spuriae* series form an important national collection

The Belsay gardens are of outstanding importance in the history of British horticulture in terms of both design and planting and are listed Grade 1. Of particular significance in the quarry garden are the rhododendrons native to the mountainous regions of the Himalaya, China, Sikkim and Assam, the largest of them planted by Sir Arthur Middleton in the early 20th century. *Rhododendron arboreum var. roseum* produces pinkish-red flowers in late November and December and the flowering sequence continues through to the large scented white flowers of *R. auriculatum* in July. In between come *R. macabeanum* (with large yellow flowers from March), *R. neriiflorum* (red flowers in March/April), *R. niveum* (purple-pink flowers in April/May), *R. barbatum* (deep red flowers in May) and the strongly scented pinkish-white flowers of *R. fortunei* (March).

Since 1999 gardeners at Belsay have been assembling a collection of species lilies. From mid-May to September these are in flower among the herbaceous borders on the terraces and alongside the paths in the quarry garden, where they are used in conjunction with shrubs to give an effect that is as natural as possible. First to flower are *Lilium pyrenaicum* (native to Europe) and *L. monadelphum* (the Caucasian lily) in the quarry garden. Also in this part of the garden are *L. wigginsii* (native to the Siskiyou Mountains of south Oregon and north California in the USA) and *L. lancefolium* (native to Japan, Korea and eastern China); the microclimate encourages *L. henryi* to grow up to 2.4m (8ft) high. Iris in the *spuriae* series form an important national collection under the National Council for the Conservation of Plants and Gardens scheme. These are located in the area of the walled gardens.

The late spring-flowering pocket-handkerchief tree (*Davidia involucrata*) and the snowbell (*Styrax japonica*), flowering in June, are just two of the more unusual trees found in the quarry garden. Magnolias also provide spring and summer interest. The winter garden is noted for its ericas; in the spring, the shrub *Osmanthus decorus* with its small, fragrant white flowers is an added attraction.

1 Rhododendron campylocarpum

2 Rhododendron rex *subspecies* fictolacteum

3 Lilium leichtlinii

4 Lilium henryi

5 Iris spuria maritima

6 Iris graminea

TERRACES

The upper terrace, on the south side of the hall, has close-mown grass to complement the austerity of the house and offers a view of the lake that is not available from the lower level. From here, steps descend to the lower terrace, which is formal and symmetrical in layout, but with deep borders and raised beds, or 'pies', planted profusely with an informal medley of shrubs and herbaceous perennials that spills over the stone kerbs onto the broad gravel walks. The beds now appear much as they did in the *Country Life* photographs of 1940.

The gardens fell into disrepair during the Second World War. In about 1944 German prisoners-of-war helped to bring them back under control and to open up pathways, which were then made of sand and had to be raked. Many of Sir Arthur Middleton's shrub plantings from about 1900 remain, notably the magnolias, and, despite this being the windiest part of the garden, the free-draining soil and southerly aspect allow the successful cultivation of more tender plants. The central group of beds has a formal arrangement of hybrid musk roses underplanted with *Alchemilla mollis* and strongly scented, old-fashioned pinks.

The view south from the terraces takes in a fine collection of rhododendrons in the middle distance, first established in the 1860s but now mostly hardy hybrids planted by Sir Arthur between 1904 and 1930. His intended colour range of red, pink, mauve and white can be appreciated from late May until mid-June. The rhododendron garden is not open to the public for conservation reasons.

YEW GARDEN

First created in the 1890s, this enclosure of clipped yew hedges with topiary finials has been re-formed since 1986 from the original trunks. The beds within the hedges are also formal, with topiary obelisks of yew providing a focus for areas of spring and summer bedding.

MAGNOLIA TERRACE

In Sir Arthur's day this broad walk was flanked on both sides by stone-edged borders. That on the north survived and now contains shrubs planted by Sir Arthur together with post-war additions by

Sir Stephen Middleton and other more recent introductions. The reinstatement of the southern border, which had been removed after the Second World War because it was regarded as too labour-intensive, began in 1996, with information provided by old *Country Life* photographs. The beds combine roses and herbaceous underplantings that spill out onto the path and butterflies can often be seen here in profusion. The summer-flowering magnolias that give the garden its name are now being replanted. A screen of evergreens enclosing the garden on the south side provides shelter, while along the northern edge a woodland of Scots pine and Douglas fir, underplanted with holly and yew, helps to maintain a Mediterranean feel appropriate to the setting of the hall.

WINTER GARDEN

This was created by Sir Arthur Middleton in the 1880s to provide lawns for croquet and tennis, essential pastimes of Victorian country-house life. At the end of the broad walk are the sunken croquet lawns, still in regular use by the local croquet club, while to the right are the borders

Above: The winter garden with its sunken croquet lawns, which are still used by the local croquet club
Left: Magnolia × weiseneri, one of the varieties providing spring and summer interest in the gardens

Facing page: The south front of the hall and the terraces, planted with a variety of shrubs and herbaceous perennials

of the winter garden, planted with a mixture of heathers, many dating back to about 1900, and flowering shrubs. Behind these are dense shrubberies, predominantly of evergreens. The western edge of this spacious enclosure is provided by a massive stone wall with Greek Revival detailing, which in summer is covered with vigorous climbing plants.

QUARRY GARDEN

By passing through the door at the end of the path around the winter garden the visitor leaves behind formality and enters an area that Sir Charles Monck intended should appear wild, romantic and even sublime. At first the path passes through an open section of wildflower meadow garden – notable for its snowdrops in early spring – framed by a quarry face to the right and mature woodland to the left. Sir Arthur introduced a number of exotic trees, notably magnolia, dogwood and the handkerchief tree, some of which have survived the taxing conditions of the quarry floor. Passing under a grove of Japanese cedars, the path enters the quarry garden proper. The feeling of enclosure is heightened by the yews and Scots pines that tower above the north cliff. The south cliff creates a shady area for a bank of native and exotic ferns, originally collected by Sir Charles. Beyond, on the left, a tall 'doorway' leads into a keyhole-shaped enclosure known as the grotto. Opposite, a small pond is fed from an underground water supply which also feeds the bog garden. The palm tree just beyond on the right is an exceptional, perhaps unique, specimen this far north.

Spanning this section, at the quarry's narrowest point, is an artificially created rock arch, introduced by Sir Charles after he had visited the quarries at Siracusa in Sicily. Beyond is a clearing ringed with cliffs and rocks, some of which are clad spectacularly with climbers. In this sunnier space rhododendrons flourish, some up to 12m (40ft) high, which flower from November to August. Some were early fruits of plant-gathering expeditions.

Sir Arthur extended the quarry garden west, creating an area where, since the recent clearance of scrub, planting is confined to native species in order to convey an impression of how the quarry appeared before the introduction of exotics. From here the path turns north through a narrowing defile, interrupted by another archway of rusticated masonry and a heavy wooden door. Beyond this the quarry narrows to 2.4m (8ft) wide; it is overhung by ivy dangling from the cliffs and wood sorrel and moss clad the many ledges. Having reached its most sublime and gloomily naturalistic point, the path emerges into a pastoral landscape, with the castle coming into view ahead.

Left: Edward Lear's The Quarries at Siracusa, *1847. The quarries inspired Sir Charles's rock arch in the quarry garden*

Facing page: The artificially created rock arch in the quarry garden

Tour of the Castle

On Christmas Day 1817, Sir Charles Monck and his family moved the short distance from Belsay Castle into the newly completed hall. The timing of this move symbolised a new beginning: the transfer of the seat of the Belsay estate from an ancient residence to a modern one. The castle dwelling gradually fell into disrepair. Its remains are still dominated by a massive late 14th-century tower. This is one of the best-surviving examples of a peel tower – a regional type of fortification built by rich families in the late Middle Ages to defend themselves during violent times on the Anglo-Scottish border.

Left: Belsay Castle in winter, seen from the south

EXTERIOR

The magnificent tower of the castle, one of the finest in Northumberland, is rectangular in plan and 70ft (21.4m) high. It is built of local sandstone and each corner is crowned by a circular turret. The ground floor has only a few very small windows but on the first floor of the south side there are two larger windows, one lighting the great chamber and the other a small room, probably a chapel. Above these windows are small carved panels, decorative details used to emphasise the importance of the rooms they light. The tower was probably added to an earlier manor house, of which nothing now survives.

Attached to the tower today are the ruins of later domestic buildings. That on the west, built in 1614, was the main range of the house and probably replaced the earlier manor house. It was entered through a porch with pairs of stout Doric columns. Above the porch door are the Middleton coat-of-arms and the inscription: THOMAS MIDDLETON AND DORATHY HIS WIFE BVILDED THIS HOUSE ANNO 1614.

Further west, another wing was added in 1711 to balance the tower. An engraving of 1728 (seen below) shows the castle at its fullest extent: with a walled forecourt, formal gardens, a walled kitchen garden and a summerhouse with a tent roof. Until 1728, when the Otterburn Turnpike (now the A696) was built on the north side of the castle,

the main road ran along the south side of the garden. A view of 1843, some 25 years after the family moved to the hall, shows the 1711 wing already dilapidated. By 1858 the estate steward was living in the rest of the house. In 1872 the ruined wing was largely pulled down and the main range of 1614 was rebuilt by Sir Arthur Middleton who wanted to create a compact, modern house, possibly as a dower house. The doorway in the porch was closed and a new entrance into the house was created to the left of it. The architects of this phase were Ross & Lamb of Darlington. Most of this part of the building is now an empty shell, the ceilings having been removed for safety reasons in 1981. The medieval tower was repaired and re-roofed in 1897.

MAIN RANGE

Visitors now enter the extension created in 1872, through the door to the left of the 1614 entrance. The remodelled hall contained a stair to the upper floor, the marks of which are preserved in the walls. To the left was the drawing room and above this a bedroom and maid's room. At first-floor level a blocked two-light window indicates the 17th-century part of the building. Inside this older section, a grate, oven and boiler show that in the 19th century the room behind the porch became a kitchen. Mr Douglas, the gamekeeper, lived here in the 1930s.

Below: Samuel and Nathaniel Buck's 1728 engraving of Belsay Castle, showing the tower on the right, the main range of 1614 in the centre and the 1711 wing to the left

Facing page: The porch to the 1614 castle extension, with the Middleton coat-of-arms above the door

CUTAWAY VIEW OF THE TOWER

Floor levels have been reconstructed

1 Main stair

2 Chapel *(probable)*

3 Kitchen

4 Well

5 Great chamber

6 Withdrawing, or bed chamber

7 The leads of the roof

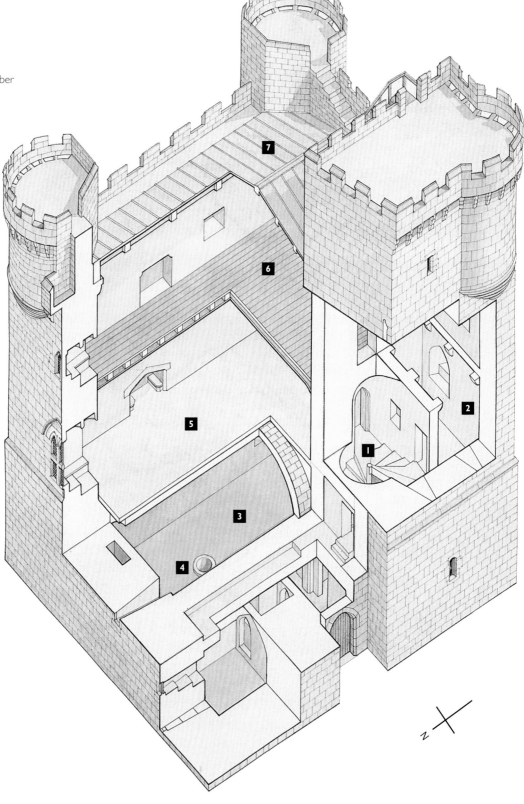

TOWER

To judge from the evidence of other sites, the tower was probably never a free-standing, self-contained residence. It is more likely to have served as a defensive stronghold and architectural centrepiece to a larger domestic complex with great hall, stables and other outbuildings – though no traces now remain. It seems probable that the tower was added to an existing manor house in response to trouble on the borders in the 14th century. The family could have retreated to the tower in times of war. There are blocked doors above the entrance at first- and second-floor levels which would once have led to the upper floors of an adjoining house.

Nothing is known for certain about the original function of the tower's interiors. It contained three principal rooms connected by a broad spiral stair that rises from a lobby at ground-floor level. There are also five smaller chambers in the south-west angle of the building. The one on the third floor has been tentatively identified as a chapel. This is due to a squint, a small internal window, which opens from the stair and would have allowed someone outside the room to see mass being celebrated at a now vanished altar. Latrines on the other side of the building on each floor open into a chute in the corner of the tower.

The main ground-floor room is barrel-vaulted and was probably a kitchen – it had a huge fireplace (now partly filled in) at its north end and a well 17ft (5m) deep (now sealed) in the floor. The door to the left of the fireplace is modern and opens through the base of the medieval latrine chute.

The timber floor of the upper chamber has been lost and the great chamber and withdrawing, or bed, chamber on the first and second floors now form a single interior rising to the roof. Both rooms have large windows and smaller closet chambers with latrines off them. They were probably withdrawing chambers for the family and the upper room may have served as a bedroom. By the 15th century the lower room was almost certainly a great chamber, a room for entertaining privileged guests. Some sense of its rich decoration is provided by the traces of medieval painting visible on the walls.

Below: Belsay Castle before the 1711 wing was demolished, by Edward Swinburne, in about 1819

The Wall Paintings

Fragments of wall plaster in the great chamber hold rare evidence for two schemes of domestic wall painting. Facing the entrance was a wild man holding a large shield.

Above: A reconstruction of how the great chamber of the castle might have looked in the late 15th century

Throughout the Middle Ages grand domestic interiors were commonly decorated with wall paintings, textiles and panelling. Today little of such early decoration survives. Fragments of wall plaster in the great chamber at Belsay Castle hold rare evidence for two superimposed schemes of domestic wall painting. These are most visible on the south and east walls. The earlier scheme, thought to date from the late 14th century, shortly after the tower was built, depicts thin, intertwining vine scrolls supporting bunches of pale pink grapes and flowers. It is bordered by stencilled flowers and simple decorative patterns. Now clear only round the window splays, it once extended across the room.

Towards the end of the 15th century the great chamber was redecorated with a new three-tier scheme. Rising from the floor is a high dado painted with a simple perspectival cube design in brown, grey and white. Along the top of this dado there existed a wooden batten, possibly a fixing for hanging decorative textiles on special occasions.

Above this is a series of heraldic shields. Most are hung on lopped trees but on the east wall, facing the entrance, a hairy figure holds a larger shield. This wild man is the supporter for the Middleton coat-of-arms. All these are set against a dark green-black field covered in delicate clusters of red and white flowers, a popular decorative motif derived from tapestries called milles fleurs.

On the south wall a narrow third tier of decoration with ships is also visible. The larger ships are carracks, three-masted vessels used in the 15th century for both merchant trading and warfare. This naval scene may be linked with the seventh Sir John Middleton, who had been twice appointed to command a fleet against the French in the 1480s. A late 15th-century date for the decoration is further supported by the surviving painted heraldry. The original coved ceiling would also have been decorated. A scheme of 14 heraldic shields painted on the great chamber ceiling was recorded in 1666 by Sir William Dugdale, though the date of their original execution is not clear.

During the early 20th century dances attended by local people were held in the castle. Although fires were not lit, the rooms were illuminated by acetylene lamps.

The spiral stair continues upwards, past more small closets, and emerges beneath a handsome eight-ribbed umbrella vault onto the roof. From here there are fine views over the surrounding parkland and countryside. Such vantage points were highly prized in the Middle Ages and the flat leads of the roof may well have been used by the Middletons and their guests for recreation. Each corner turret contains a vaulted closet at roof level. The crenellations on the south have moulded edges, suggesting that this was the most important side of the building.

OUTBUILDINGS: STABLES & KENNELS

Running north from the castle, but not physically connected to it until the 19th century, is a two-storey range. The masonry of the building suggests that it is a medieval structure, though its original function is uncertain. At the far end is the office court, with a fine range of 18th-century stables along the west and simple single-storey kennels on the east, designed by Sir Charles Monck in the early 19th century.

At the far end of the court is a gate with a view across the park to an ornamental building called Bantam Folly (not in the care of English Heritage), acting in part as an eyecatcher. The exact date of the building is uncertain but it was in existence by 1769. The detail is Georgian Gothick, with a crenellated parapet and a quatrefoil, or four-lobed, window opening into a pigeon loft, so possibly it was originally a utilitarian farm building that was subsequently adapted to provide a feature in the landscape. Until the mid-20th century it sported a wooden spire, which made it resemble a church.

From the path leading back towards the car park, the broad 'hot walls' (not open to the public) built by Sir Charles Monck in the kitchen garden can be seen across the field to the left. These walls with internal flues were used for growing exotic fruits and plants. Two sections have been reinstated and fruit trees replanted on them, although the walls are not now heated.

Left: Bantam Folly in the 1970s, before its restoration. Probably once a farm building, it was adapted to provide an ornamental feature in the landscape

History

The Middletons have lived at Belsay since 1270. After Sir Richard de Middleton became Henry III's Lord Chancellor in 1269, none of them rose to national prominence; most generations held county office and married into other Northumbrian families. Belsay is nonetheless remarkable for the architectural and horticultural legacy of the extraordinary Sir Charles Middleton who changed his name to Monck in 1796.

READING THE HISTORY

This section describes the history of the castle, hall and gardens up to the present. Short biographies of Sir Charles Monck and Sir Arthur Middleton are included, together with features on the Greek Revival (page 41) and the Picturesque Movement (page 42).

THE EARLY MIDDLETONS AND THE BUILDING OF THE CASTLE

The Belsay estate has been in the possession of the Middleton family almost continuously since the 13th century. It is first recorded in 1270, when it was known as Beleshou and was owned by Sir Richard de Middleton. Lord Chancellor to King Henry III from 1269 until his death in 1272, he was the only member of the family in seven centuries to become prominent nationally.

In 1317 Middleton's nephew Gilbert, prompted by the regional anarchy that followed Edward II's defeat by the Scots at the Battle of Bannockburn in 1314, led a rising of local men. They held to ransom two cardinals who were travelling to Scotland on a diplomatic mission, extorted a large sum from the powerful Bishop of Durham and plundered southwards into Yorkshire. There the men deserted and Gilbert and his cousin John, heir to Sir Richard, were captured by troops loyal to the king. They met a traitor's fate in London by being hanged, drawn and quartered. The Belsay estate was then forfeited and granted to a succession of owners, finally returning to the Middleton family by marriage in 1391. Since then it has never left their ownership, although the nucleus of the estate with the castle and hall was transferred to the guardianship of the state in 1980.

There is no known documentary evidence for the date of the castle's tower but it can be deduced through the evidence of an armorial stone that once decorated the south side of the building. This displayed the arms of the Stryvelyns and Middletons, celebrating the marriage between the two families that eventually restored the Belsay estates to the Middletons some 70 years after they had been confiscated. The evidence of the armorial stone suggests that John Middleton built the tower between his marriage in 1391 and his death in 1396. It seems likely that John envisaged the tower at Belsay as a celebration of this momentous event for the Middleton family, as well as a prudent defensive measure during this violent period of border conflict.

THE MIDDLETONS IN LATER CENTURIES

From the late 14th century until the early 17th the Middletons continued to live in the castle, holding local official and military appointments along the border. In 1614 Thomas Middleton

redeveloped the castle, adding an ambitious Jacobean range, one of the first completely undefended domestic buildings in the county. Several castles in the area underwent similar alteration in this period, including nearby Chipchase. Nearly a century later a west wing was added in a plain Georgian style, visually counterbalancing the medieval tower; this probably dated from 1711 – the date given on a sundial from this building – and was largely demolished in the early 19th century.

Thomas Middleton's son was created a baronet in 1662. It was the fifth baronet, Sir William Middleton, who embarked in the second half of the 18th century on landscaping improvements in the manner made fashionable by Lancelot 'Capability' Brown (died 1783). These included new informal planting, a serpentine drive that meandered through the park towards the castle – crossing a bridge over a newly formed lake – and the development of Bantam Folly as a Gothick eyecatcher to the west of the castle. Many of these features are shown on an estate map drawn up in 1792.

From top: Joseph Wright of Derby's portraits, 1760, of Mr and Mrs Lawrence Monck, grandparents of Sir Charles, and their daughter Jane (left), mother of Sir Charles and wife of the fifth baronet, Sir William Middleton

Facing page: The spiral staircase in the castle, in Country Life, 1940

SIR CHARLES MONCK

The man who made by far the greatest impact on Belsay was Sir William's third son, Charles, the sixth baronet. Born in 1779, he became heir apparent to the estate at the age of 10, after the deaths of his two older brothers. The family had recently been enriched by the inheritance of coal-bearing land in Durham and south Northumberland, an estate in Essex and business interests in London and Edinburgh. On his father's death in 1795, Charles inherited everything at the age of 16. The following year he was obliged to adopt the surname of his rich grandfather Lawrence Monck, a self-made London merchant, as a condition of additionally inheriting the latter's estate in Lincolnshire. He returned to Belsay and quickly established himself as such a diligent manager of the estate that, despite being a minor, the Lord Chancellor appointed Charles receiver of his own property. This attention to duty remained one of his distinguishing characteristics for the rest of his life.

Sir Charles had been educated at Rugby School, and, although he was removed at the age of 15 when the headmaster went mad, he had evidently acquired during his time there a passion for the Classics and Greek in particular. When, in 1804, he married his cousin Louisa Cooke of Doncaster, he chose Greece for the honeymoon. War with Napoleon placed France and Italy out of bounds, so when the couple set off on 11 September they travelled from Harwich to Denmark. They then made their way via Berlin – where Sir Charles sketched the Brandenburg Gate, a building then just 10 years old – Dresden, Prague, Vienna, Trieste and Venice, to Athens, where they finally arrived in May 1805. Lady Monck gave birth to a son there that summer. He was given the names 'Charles Atticus', the second name being a reflection of his father's infatuation with Greece. Meanwhile, Sir Charles passed the summer in expeditions to various ancient sites, often in the company of Sir William Gell, another Englishman with a keen interest in Greek architecture and archaeology. He sketched what he saw and, in some cases, as at the Parthenon and the Theseion in Athens, he took careful measurements. In October the Moncks began the slow journey home, travelling by sea and eventually arriving at Belsay on 5 April 1806.

Despite concerning himself so closely with the design of the hall and gardens at Belsay and despite his apparently obsessive admiration for Greece and its ancient remains, architecture does not otherwise seem to have been a particular passion of Sir Charles's. Unlike other gentlemen-architects he did not make a habit of designing houses for others: the sum total of his output, apart from Belsay Hall, was the much less remarkable Linden Hall to the north of Morpeth (built in 1811–12 and now a hotel), and a number of small functional buildings on his own estates, including the replacement village at Belsay. Although during his honeymoon in Greece he had spent some time in the company of other like-minded Hellenophiles such as Gell, once back in Northumberland he reverted to the social world of family and country-house society. He travelled widely on the Continent again, in the 1830s, recording what he saw in his diaries and notebooks. He was above all, however, a patriot for his own region: he noted in 1831 of Durham Cathedral that 'its superiority over anything which I have seen on the Continent is immeasurable'. He was in fact just as likely to make a note of birds or trees he had seen, or the earliest peaches and latest strawberries eaten, as he was to make architectural observations. As far as architecture was concerned he had a clear dislike of anything showy, whether it was the extravagant gestures of the Baroque, or the bright and – to his eyes – clashing shades of Continental colour schemes (his own preferences, in evidence at Belsay, were for green and grey).

He had an enquiring mind, especially in matters of modern technology, and he approached his own responsibilities as a rich and prominent country gentleman with great conscientiousness. He had a dutiful, if undistinguished, Parliamentary career as Whig MP for the county of Northumberland, attending the House of Commons regularly and indeed acquiring a reputation as a nuisance by addressing the House at length in Greek. He was equally dogged in performing his duties as magistrate over many years, although one local contemporary noted that 'no-one paid much attention to anything he said'.

Above: Sir William Gell (1777–1836) who visited ancient sites with Sir Charles
Top left: An extract from Sir Charles's diary, with his sketch of the Brandenburg Gate in Berlin
Below left: An extract from Sir Charles's diary, including one of his sketches of ancient Greek sculpture

Facing page, above: Sir Charles in 1865, at the age of 86. He refused to have his portrait painted but was interested in the 'new medium of photography'
Facing page, below: Belsay village, for which Sir Charles designed a number of buildings, as seen in this early 20th-century postcard

THE NEW HALL

Above: The interior of Longhirst Hall, near Morpeth (1824), designed by John Dobson and influenced by Belsay

THE NEW HALL

On his return from honeymoon Sir Charles quickly set about designing a new house, drawing on what he had seen in Greece and during his other travels, on his collection of architectural books, and possibly on English country houses that he had visited or seen illustrated. It has been remarked that although he could have found what he required for the design in various architectural publications, he felt that he needed to have visited Greece to secure the 'authentic' feel. The result is a fascinating synthesis of sources and influences, the more remarkable because he had no training as an architect and his circle of acquaintance contained no-one of that profession. Although the Greek Revival had effectively been introduced in Britain in a garden temple designed for Hagley Hall in Worcestershire by James 'Athenian' Stuart in 1758, there were still in 1806 few precedents for a substantial country house in the style.

Sir Charles adopted the massive baseless Doric columns that he had seen on the Theseion, but since he knew that in ancient Greece projecting porticos were restricted to temples and never used on secular buildings, he used the columns instead to create a portico *in antis* on the entrance front of the mansion. This feature had been used occasionally on early 18th-century English houses and been revived by neoclassical architects such as Sir William Chambers and Sir John Soane towards the end of the century. But nobody had designed a country-house exterior so massive and uncompromisingly austere, so devoid of extraneous ornament.

For the plan of the hall Sir Charles could not draw on ancient Greek precedent, since nothing remotely suitable existed. His inspiration was more that of the ancient Roman villa with a central courtyard, as modified for the northern climate by 18th-century English architects such as James Paine and Sir Robert Taylor; the latter's Purbrook House in Hampshire of 1770, with its colonnaded top-lit atrium, has been suggested as one likely source. Belsay is a rare example of a house in which the influence of the Antique dominates both the appearance and the plan. The use of smooth-cut stone for both the exterior and the 'public' parts of the interior – the entrance hall and Pillar Hall – also had recent precedents in the work of Soane. There were never many clients prepared to accept the chill severity that inevitably accompanied it, but it became more commonly used in subsequent houses of the Greek Revival. Much as his neighbours might admire Sir Charles's strength of character in the design and building of the hall and Lady Monck's forbearance in living there, Belsay was never likely to attract many imitators. It is the special quality of Belsay that everything – plan, elevations, detailing, proportion – is subjected to a ruthless rationality such as architects can rarely impose on their clients but which the gentleman-architect could impose on himself and on his long-suffering family.

Its main architectural influence was on John Dobson (1787–1865), who as a young man may have assisted in drawing the Ionic capitals for the Pillar Hall and became a prolific architect in the region. Among the many houses he designed for the newly rich of early 19th-century Newcastle, a number adopt the same basic layout as Belsay, with central top-lit halls, staircases opening off to one side, reception rooms arranged along the south front and servants' quarters in a wing to the north – Longhirst Hall near Morpeth, of 1824, is perhaps the best surviving example. The now demolished Cresswell Hall on the Northumberland coast (1821–5) was the closest imitation, built by John Shaw who had visited Belsay in 1811.

On a purely practical level the influence of Belsay in the region was considerable. Sir Charles demanded the highest standards of workmanship from the craftsmen he employed. While a small number were from London – the upholsterer Edward Bailey, the brazier William Collins and the locksmith Bramah – most were local and, indeed, were already working on the estate when Sir Charles inherited it in 1795. Although he is said to have rejected Sir William Gell's suggestion that stone caryatids be used in the central hall on the grounds that local carvers would not be up to it, Sir Charles nevertheless managed to coax extraordinarily fine results from them when it came to cutting and laying the stone for the walls and columns. Dobson later stated that the dispersal of the masons who had worked at Belsay 'much raised the standard of good mason work in the north of England'.

The Greek Revival

Interest in the architectural remains of the Roman Empire in the West formed the basis of the Renaissance revival of classicism. But ancient Greek remains in both Greece and Asia Minor were little known, being part of the Ottoman Empire and hazardous to reach. It was not until the mid-18th century that an effort was made to record ancient Greek monuments and to imitate them in contemporary buildings. In 1751, sponsored by the Society of Dilettanti in London, a gentleman's club combining heavy drinking with a serious interest in the past, James Stuart and Nicholas Revett spent three years drawing and measuring monuments in Greece. The first volume of their massive *The Antiquities of Athens* (1762) launched the Greek Revival in Britain and earned Stuart the nickname 'Athenian'. His laziness, though, meant that Volume II was published posthumously in 1789 and Volume V appeared only in 1830. This, and opposition from promoters of 'Roman' classicism, such as Robert Adam and Sir William Chambers, meant that the Revival was slow to achieve popularity. At first Greek influence was seen mainly in garden buildings. It was not until after 1800 that it appeared in country houses; an early example is The Grange in Hampshire, recast in 1808–9 to resemble a Greek temple. The style could seem austere in the British climate and was more popular for public buildings, the British Museum (1823–46) and National Gallery (1834–8) in London being prominent examples. In the North-East the Moot Hall (1810) in Newcastle, by John Stokoe, was one of the first occurrences of the Greek Revival and John Dobson, the leading local architect, used the style widely.

James 'Athenian' Stuart was sponsored by the Society of Dilettanti, a private gentleman's club which combined heavy drinking with a serious interest in the past.

Above: James 'Athenian' Stuart (1713–88), in a portrait of the 1760s attributed to Philip Jean
Left: The Grange in Hampshire (also in the care of English Heritage) – an early example of a Greek Revival country house

The Picturesque Movement

There was an upsurge in travel to areas such as the Peak and Lake Districts and Wales, previously regarded as wild and uncivilised but now greatly valued for the same reasons. A taste for ruins led to many being created from scratch, which is why follies sprang up on hilltops all over the country.

The Picturesque movement emerged in 18th-century England as an aesthetic concept in which gardens and landscapes were viewed as pictorial compositions, as seen through the eyes of 17th-century artists such as Claude Lorraine, Salvator Rosa and Ruysdael.

The development of the Picturesque led to the owners of estates remodelling them in a 'picturesque' manner, heightening any dramatic potential wherever possible. It also encouraged an upsurge in travel to areas such as the Peak and Lake Districts and Wales, previously regarded as wild and uncivilised but now greatly valued for the same reasons.

The bland beauty of 'Capability' Brown's earlier formula of smooth turf, artificial lakes and careful clumps of trees gave way to a preference for the rugged, cliffs and gorges, rushing streams, ruins and sublimity. Hawkstone in Shropshire is an early example of a Georgian park which consciously exploited natural topography by being extended to include cliffs, rocks and a medieval ruin. If necessary, such features could be created from scratch, which is why follies or eyecatchers sprang up on hilltops all over the country.

William Gilpin popularised the term Picturesque in his writings in the 1780s and the criteria were elaborated by Uvedale Price in his *Essay on the Picturesque* (1794). Price believed the key points were roughness, sudden variation and irregularity. His friend Richard Payne Knight added to the debate (followed with keen interest by the educated public) with his poem *The Landscape*, also published in 1794. He attacked the landscaping approach of Brown and his successor Humphry Repton and emphasised the need for 'the stately mansion' to be just one component in a varied pictorial composition. These lessons were all taken to heart at Belsay by Sir Charles Monck.

Right: Grotto with Cascades by Salvator Rosa, 17th century
Far right: Detail of portrait of Richard Payne Knight (c 1793–4), by Sir Thomas Lawrence

CREATING THE QUARRY GARDEN

Although his father had done much to bring the surroundings of the castle into line with the latest trends in landscaping advocated by 'Capability' Brown (died 1783), fashions had moved on again by the time Sir Charles began work on the hall. The Picturesque movement then in vogue advocated the shaping of landscapes less blandly beautiful and more craggily naturalistic. This was often a problem in the lowland south of England, but the North offered greater scope. The terrain at Belsay was predominantly fairly gentle and there was not much that could be done to the north and east of the new house other than to extend the 18th-century parkland, with its artful dotting of trees and with a ha-ha to create the impression of grass sweeping uninterrupted up to the entrance front. To the south, however, the house looked over a valley to a rocky hillside, which Sir Charles planted with a mixture of newly introduced exotic conifers, Scots pines and native hardwoods. In combination these provided a sombre backdrop to the new lake in the bottom of the valley, with its little cascade, and a distinct contrast to the adjoining parkland. In the middle ground was a broom-covered hillock where Sir Charles experimented with growing monkey-puzzle trees, while in the immediate foreground of the house he took a leaf out of Humphry Repton's book by introducing formal terraces supported on a massive arcaded wall.

Sir Charles showed himself to be a true original to the west of the hall. Here a wood of Scots pines and Douglas firs gave shelter from northerly winds to a broad terrace walk with parallel borders of brightly coloured annuals, which introduced (on sunny summer days at least) a surprisingly Mediterranean note. Beyond began the romantic quarry garden that is still Belsay's greatest claim to horticultural fame. Although created by the purely practical necessity of extracting enough stone to build the hall, the quarry was excavated with great care and to Sir Charles's predetermined plan of making a dramatic canyon, rather than just a large hole in the ground. The scale of the garden was enhanced by planting yews and pines along the top of the northern cliff, while down in the quarry the vegetation was largely 'natural' and mainly of native

plants, at least initially (though the Chusan palm, *Trachycarpus fortunei*, is one of the earliest examples in Britain). Here the pictorial inspiration is the sublime landscapes depicted in the paintings of Salvator Rosa (1615–73); but late-Georgian gentlemen and ladies could stand only so much drama and sublimity and were provided with the well-tended paths necessary for easy perambulation.

THE WALLED KITCHEN GARDEN

In addition to the ornamental gardens, Sir Charles developed a walled kitchen garden to the north-west of the hall. Even there he was innovative and introduced a heated wall and ranges of hot-houses for growing exotic fruits. There were specialist horticultural buildings, such as a mushroom house and apple store, so that a wide range of fruit and vegetables could be grown and stored on site for use in the hall. Although some of these buildings were demolished in the late 19th century, the major features of Sir Charles's walled gardens, including the heated wall, survive.

Left: Sketch by J Liddell of the quarry garden at Belsay, 19th century
Below: The quarry garden in Country Life, *1940*

SIR ARTHUR MIDDLETON'S CONTRIBUTION

When Sir Charles died in 1867 at the great age of 88, he was succeeded by his grandson Arthur (as his son Charles Atticus Monck had died in 1856). In 1876 Sir Arthur changed his surname from Monck back to Middleton.

He employed in 1897 the architect Charles Ferguson to restore and re-roof the castle, in the process removing the evidence for post-medieval changes: in the 1870s Sir Arthur had demolished the Georgian west range and rebuilt the 1614 house. He did relatively little to the hall, beyond remodelling the reception rooms to either side of the library in the years before the First World War, with careful attention to his grandfather's original drawings.

Sir Arthur was more interventionist in the gardens, but again he respected his grandfather's concept, especially in the quarry garden. Sir Charles had certainly been interested in plants but his grandson was a true plantsman, making full use of the many new species being introduced into England during the late 19th century. His grandfather disliked strong colours, but Sir Arthur took advantage of the introductions to brighten up the gardens. He massed hardy hybrid rhododendrons in the valley below the terraces on the south side of the hall and diversified the planting in the quarry garden with more colourful and exotic

Above: Sir Arthur Middleton
in the quarry garden,
about 1900

Below: The Middleton children
enjoying a sleigh ride in front
of the Belsay stable block,
about 1910

Facing page: The wedding
of Hugh and Mary Middleton
in 1905

species. The softening of the planting in the formal terrace borders reduced the contrast with the informal quarry garden and left the hall looking even more uncompromisingly severe. Between the hall and quarry he created the yew garden, enclosed by clipped hedges and topiary, and the winter garden, with lawns for croquet and tennis. The latter was bounded emphatically on its western edge by a massive stone wall with Grecian detail. His main contribution to the quarry was to introduce further trees, shrubs and climbers, and in particular species rhododendrons. Perennials were naturalised in the grass, colonising the quarry floor, and deciduous flowering trees were planted around the meadow. The pond and the second arch in the quarry garden also belong to Sir Arthur's period. Around the castle he planted more ornamental trees and in front of it an elaborate garden, typical of the late 19th century.

During the whole of Sir Arthur's 66-year tenure of the estate quarrying took place alongside Sir Charles's quarry garden, on the site of the vanished medieval village and the 18th-century kitchen garden. Stone was still extracted into the 1930s. In the process another L-shaped canyon was created in much the same Picturesque spirit as the first, varying deliberately in width and with wings of rock projecting from either side to break its length into a succession of compartments.

Memories of Belsay

To feel the warm welcome, to mount the stairs, candlestick in hand and see the flickering shadows of the candlelight on all the pillars was glory.

In the 1990s Priscilla Napier, née Hayter (above) recalled her memories of visiting Belsay in the 1920s when young:

'There was snow everywhere, as I and my brother William Hayter were driven from Newcastle station by Robert Best, head-groom-cum-chauffeur, for a fortnight at Belsay with the Middletons. To one more used to the elmy meadows of southern England, Belsay came as an incredible surprise – the snowy, cold landscape without, and the generous warmth within; arrival at that magnificently unique four-square house with its leaping fires, standing so boldly forth in its surround of sparkling snow. To feel the warm welcome, to mount the stairs, candlestick in hand and see the flickering shadows of the candlelight on all the pillars, to find the hip-bath on its bath mat spread beside the blazing fire in one's bedroom, was glory.

'It was demonstrably a happy home, presided over by Sir Arthur Middleton, who knew everything there was to be known about Northumberland. Dwelling mainly in his study on the south-east corner of the house, he emerged to take the head of the table at mealtimes and to contribute a quota of his erudition to the less learned and noisier conversation of his grandchildren. There was a lunchtime in the summer holidays, when Sir Arthur arose abruptly, announced that he could not abide hooligan manners and left the dining room with his dignified step as a protest against the noise. After this a repentant silence followed, during which people picked up their fallen napkins and sat straighter, eating raspberry tart in a subdued fashion. I do not think that anyone after this rolled silver pepper-pots at one another across the table again.'

BELSAY IN THE 20TH CENTURY

In the early 20th century, life at the hall continued much as it had ever done, with the Middletons entertaining their county neighbours supported by a substantial staff. Money was not as plentiful as it had been, however, and Sir Arthur made the gardens more low-maintenance through the use of perennials and heathers; he also reduced the amount of labour deployed in the kitchen garden.

During the Second World War the hall was occupied by the Army and the gardens ceased to be maintained. The fine furniture was stored in the attics and the servants' quarters were used for the ordinary soldiers. The library became the officers' lounge (the chimneypiece was boarded up, though not before some of the soldiers had scratched their names on it). As with so many country houses, this military interlude was the beginning of the end for Belsay's domestic use; although the Middleton family returned after the War it was neither an easy nor a comfortable building in which to live in reduced circumstances. In 1962 Sir Stephen Middleton, the ninth baronet, decided to move to Swanstead, a smaller and more manageable house on the estate. He died in 1994. Auctions had dissipated much of the historic contents and dry rot began to infest the empty mansion.

The hall, together with the castle and historic nucleus of the estate, was transferred to the guardianship of the state in 1980. This was followed by extensive stripping of the internal wood and plasterwork after the discovery of an outbreak of dry rot in rooms on the north front. Much of the damp had been caused by the internal drain system installed by Sir Charles Monck in order to ensure that functional guttering and piping would not detract from the grandeur and austerity of the building's exterior. The extensive removal of original architectural fittings, coupled with repairs to the roof, eradicated the damp but left much of the building as an empty shell. In 2000 English Heritage took the decision to replace floors in the anteroom, housekeeper's room and estate office on the ground floor and in Sir Charles Monck's bedroom on the first floor. Where possible, those fittings that were salvaged from the stripping out of the 1980s were reinstated and key rooms on the first floor were repaired. In due course, rooms of the service wing, the mezzanine bedrooms and servants' accommodation will be reinstated. Since the 1980s the formal gardens have been restored to their appearance in the 1920s and 1930s. In the quarries and informal parts of the garden, Sir Arthur's plantings are now fully mature and Picturesque in their effect. The aim here has been to maintain that effect but using exotic plants, while Sir Arthur's west quarry, which had reverted to scrub, will continue to house purely native plants in order to show the style of the quarry garden before the exotic introductions.

Right: The north front of the hall in 1973, before being taken into guardianship

CONTEMPORARY BELSAY

The fact that Belsay Hall came to English Heritage
unfurnished – and with a proviso that it should
continue to be presented to the public in
this state – has provided the opportunity of
interpreting Belsay in a different way – through
contemporary design. These summer exhibitions
have been produced by Arts Council England
North East and English Heritage and have
received financial support from regional partners.

The first, in 1996, brought together more than
200 examples of modern textiles, silver, glass and
furniture in a show entitled 'Living at Belsay'. It was
inspired by the enthusiasm of the designer Jean
Muir, who had a great love of Northumberland
and of Belsay in particular. This was followed in
2000 by 'Sitooteries', a display of contemporary
interpretations of traditional summerhouses.

The 2004 exhibition, 'Fashion At Belsay', spread
beyond the rooms of the hall to the grounds and
the castle, with installations by fashion designers
such as Alexander McQueen, Stella McCartney
and Zandra Rhodes. For 'Picture House' (2007)
film directors, sound and music producers, actors,
artists and fashion designers transformed Belsay,
filling empty spaces with installations featuring
sound, smell and animation. In one room a tree
grew out of a bed; another was filled with 2000
teacups. All these exhibitions have brought the
long tradition of innovative design at Belsay into
the 21st century.

Above: Viktor & Rolf's
installation in the Pillar Hall
during the 2007 'Picture
House' exhibition
Left: Geraldine Pilgrim's
installation featuring 2000
teacups exhibited during
'Picture House'
Far left: Lucky Spot by
Stella McCartney, one
of the works exhibited in
'Fashion at Belsay'

Belsay's historic landscape

The nucleus of Belsay Park lay between Belsay Castle and an Iron Age fort on Bantam Hill to the west. Sir William Middleton began to turn the Park into an ornamental landscape from 1764, but it was his son, Sir Charles Monck, who transformed it, creating Belsay Hall, three lodges, gardens, a new lake and village buildings, including an inn and school.

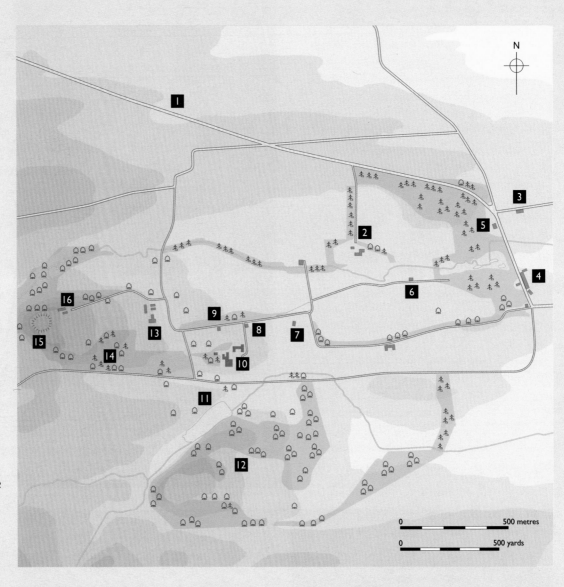

AREA MAP

1 Otterburn Turnpike (A696), 1746–52, extended 1831

2 Swanstead, probably 1771, rebuilt in 1946–7 for Sir Stephen Middleton *(private)*

3 Former school, 1835 *(private)*

4 Belsay village. The original village was relocated in 1831. Sir Charles designed and built Belsay Arcade, inspired by arcaded streets in Italy

5 Former Castle Inn, 1836 *(private)*

6 Old Boathouse, 1789, at Belsay Lough, a lake which was infilled by Sir Charles

7 Hall Field Lodge, 1830s *(private)*

8 Hall Lodge, 1830s *(private)*

9 Garden House, 1837 *(private)*

10 Belsay Hall and stables

11 Lake, by 1840

12 Crag Wood *(for walk, see page 21)*

13 Castle, kennels and stables

14 Quarry garden

15 Iron Age hillfort

16 Bantam Folly, built by 1769 by Sir William Middleton *(private)*